EXTREME

Pets
Parents
Hate!

Animal Life Cycles

Trevor Day

Capstone
press®

Mankato, Minnesota

W9-AWZ-622

Fact Finders is published by Capstone Press,
a Capstone Publishers company.
151 Good Counsel Drive, P.O. Box 669,
Mankato, Minnesota 56002.
www.capstonepress.com

First published 2008
Copyright © 2008 A & C Black Publishers Limited

Produced for A & C Black by
     Monkey Puzzle Media Ltd
     The Rectory, Eyke, Woodbridge
     Suffolk IP12 2QW, UK

No part of this publication may be reproduced in whole
or in part, or stored in a retrieval system, or transmitted
in any form or by any means, electronic, mechanical,
photocopying, recording, or otherwise, without written
permission of the publisher.
For information regarding permission, write to Capstone
Press, 151 Good Counsel Drive, P.O. Box 669, Dept. R,
Mankato, Minnesota 56002.

The right of Trevor Day to be identified as the author of
this Work has been asserted by him in accordance with
the Copyright, Designs and Patents Act 1988.

Library of Congress Cataloging-in-Publication Data

Day, Trevor.
    Pets parents hate! : animal life cycles / by Trevor
Day.
        p. cm. -- (Fact finders: Extreme!)
    Includes bibliographical references and index.
    Summary: "Presents unusual pets and their care,
including life cycle information"--Provided by
publisher.
    ISBN-13: 978-1-4296-3109-9 (hardcover)
    ISBN-10: 1-4296-3109-0 (hardcover)
    ISBN-13: 978-1-4296-3129-7 (softcover pbk.)
    ISBN-10: 1-4296-3129-5 (softcover pbk.)
    ISBN-13: 978-1-4296-6487-5 (softcover pbk.)
    1. Pets--Juvenile literature. 2. Wild animals as pets--
Juvenile literature. 3. Animal life cycles--Juvenile literature.
I. Title. II. Series.

SF416.2.D35 2009
636.088'7--dc22

2008023571

Editor: Cath Senker
Design: Mayer Media Ltd
Picture research: Lynda Lines
Series consultant: Jane Turner

This book is produced using paper that is made from
wood grown in managed, sustainable forests. It is natural,
renewable, and recyclable. The logging and manufacturing
processes conform to the environmental regulations of
the country of origin.

Printed in China, 072010, 005866

Picture acknowledgements
Alamy p. 25 top (Arco Images); Corbis pp. 1 (Jeffrey L
Rotman), 10 (Tom Brakefield), 15 (Tim Davis), 24 (Jeffrey
L Rotman); FLPA pp. 7 (Mark Moffett/ Minden Pictures),
11 (Mark Moffett/Minden Pictures), 13 (Nigel Cattlin),
19 (Chris Mattison), 23 (Angela Hampton), 25 bottom
(Michael Krabs/Imagebroker), 29 (RP Lawrence); Getty
Images pp. 8–9 (Frank Greenaway), 28 (AFP); iStockphoto
pp. 5 (Holly Kuchera), 6, 14 (Feng Yu); NHPA p. 20
(Anthony Bannister); Photographers Direct p. 16 (Helena
Kadlcikova); Photolibrary.com pp. 12, 17 (E. Degginger),
18 (Vivek Sinha); Rex Features p. 27 (Geoff Moore);
RSPCA Photolibrary p. 22 (Angela Hampton); Science
Photo Library pp. 4 (David Aubrey), 21 top (M.H. Sharp),
26 (Alan Carey); Still Pictures p. 21 bottom (Biosphoto/
Gunther Michel).

The front cover shows a Mexican red-knee tarantula
(Getty Images/Brian Stablyk).

Every effort has been made to contact copyright holders
of material reproduced in this book. Any omissions will be
rectified in subsequent printings if notice is given to the

CONTENTS

Disclaimer
None of these pets should be kept without adult supervision. As will become clear, some of these animals should not be kept as pets at all.

Abbreviations **m** stands for meters • **ft** stands for feet • **in** stands for inches •
cm stands for centimeters • **g** stands for grams • **lb** stands for pounds

Pets parents hate

Several million types of animals live on the planet. They range from tiny ants to whales as big as aircraft. A few thousand kinds are kept as pets. Some make better housemates than others.

Venomous (poisonous) sting used to kill **prey** and to defend itself

Parents will probably hate dangerous pets, such as scorpions. Most will certainly dislike smelly skunks. Even cute pets take up space. They all need food, water, and a safe, comfortable place to live.

The maps in this book show where each animal comes from.

Some people keep imperial scorpions, like this one, as pets.

Claws for grabbing prey

prey a creature that is eaten by other creatures

Pet skunks are active and love to play. They need plenty of attention. When scared, a skunk arches its back and lifts its tail to make itself look bigger. If it is very frightened, it squirts stinky **fluid** from two openings near its tail.

The black bear cub has frightened the skunk. The cub may get a smelly surprise!

Stinking skunks

The scientific name for a skunk is *Mephitis mephitis*, meaning "stinks, stinks."

fluid a liquid; a runny substance

Praying mantis: the Kung Fu fighter

What does an insect have to do with humans fighting? One style of Kung Fu is based on the moves of the praying mantis.

The praying mantis gets its name because its front legs look like they are being held out in prayer. The insect strikes its prey by whipping its front legs forward. It stabs the victim's weakest parts. Then the praying mantis eats its victim alive. The insect's moves inspired Wang Lang, one of the people who created Kung Fu.

Pet praying mantises should be kept alone in a tank. Otherwise they will attack each other.

Live prey

A pet praying mantis needs live insects, such as flies or grasshoppers, to eat. You can buy them from a pet shop— or catch them yourself.

A praying mantis should be kept among plants so that it can hide.

Large eyes for finding prey

Front legs for stabbing

STAB!

Body shape and color help the mantis hide among leaves and branches.

STAB!

An African praying mantis, close up.

A mantis hides and waits silently for its prey to come within stabbing range.

insect a six-legged animal with a hard outer skeleton and a body divided into three parts

How many legs?
Millipedes and centipedes

Millipedes and centipedes both have many legs. The biggest animals grow to about 10 inches (25 centimeters) long. One of them bites. The other does not. Which is which?

Peruvian giant orange leg centipede

A lot of legs

Millipedes (from the Latin for "thousand legs") in fact have between 100 and 700 legs. Centipedes ("hundred legs") have between 30 and 160.

Hard, glossy outer skeleton gives protection

Large body segments

One pair of legs for each **segment**

segment a repeated main part of the body

Antennae for sensing smells and vibrations in the dark

Before you decide to have a pet, you should find out about the animal. Millipedes make good pets. They feed on bits of dead plants and animals. When frightened, they curl up.

Big centipedes are not such good pets. They are predators—they hunt other animals. Centipedes inject **venom** into their prey with their fangs to overpower it. They could bite you, too!

Ouch!
Fangs inject venom

Joints between each segment allow the body to bend.

venom poison

Hairy housemates: tarantulas

Sting shocks

Imagine your mom or dad opening the curtains to find a large, hairy tarantula staring them in the face. Is your poor parent in danger?

In fact, tarantulas can make great pets, if you choose the right type and treat them carefully. If a tarantula bites you, it is usually no worse than a wasp sting.

Some types of tarantulas live on the ground, while others prefer trees. Some are **solitary**, but others live in groups. Check so you can give the tarantula the right surroundings and food. It will eat crickets, mealworms, large flies, or even small dead mice.

A few people are **allergic** to tarantula bites. They may go into shock and even stop breathing. An injection of a drug called adrenaline stops the shock.

The Chilean rose tarantula is a solitary, ground-living spider. Tarantulas can grow to the size of a man's hand.

---

allergic become ill when the body reacts badly to a particular substance **solitary** living alone

The pink-toed tarantula is a social, tree-living spider.

1 This spider has caught a bat.

4 The spider then sucks them up like soup.

SUCKS UP

VENOM IN

2 The spider injects venom through its fangs to stun its prey.

3 The venom also **digests** the insides of the bat.

digests breaks down into substances the body can use

On the trail of a snail

You'll know where a pet snail has been from the glistening slimy trail that it leaves behind. This will not make your parents happy.

African land snails with their young

Fast breeder

Every snail is both male and female. Any two adults can **fertilize** each other. They can each lay several hundred eggs in a year.

fertilize when a sperm joins with an egg to make a new individual

Some people love keeping African land snails as pets because they look so strange. Their body changes shape, they hide inside the shell, or they stretch out and slide around. These snails are not allowed into the United States in case they escape, breed, and munch crops. They have a giant appetite for juicy leaves.

The giant African land snail can grow to more than 6 in (15 cm) long and weigh a massive 1 lb (450 g).

A snail needs to eat plenty of calcium to make its chalky shell. Egg shells or **cuttlebone** can provide this.

Uh-oh!
The snail hides in its spiral shell when threatened.

Slime!
Mucus trail

Scratchy!
Rough tongue shreds leafy food

Tentacles (eyes on stalks)

cuttlebone skeleton of a cuttlefish   **mucus** slime made by animals

Piranhas: like a bite?

Piranha fish have teeth that cut like sharp scissors. Some people say that a shoal of piranhas can strip a living horse or human to the bone in minutes. Is this the kind of fish you'd like to keep in your bedroom?

Don't keep your piranha with smaller fish. It will eat them!

Piranhas are not really as scary as they seem. Even starving piranhas rarely attack large animals. Very few horses and people have ever been killed in this way—but it has happened. Piranhas usually live in South American rivers. They nip the scales and fins of larger fish and feed on dead animals. Piranhas also eat plants.

You can keep a piranha as a pet in a tank of clean, warm, fresh (not salty) water at 75–83°F (24–28°C). Make sure it has places to hide. You should feed it fish food and sometimes offer fresh vegetables. Remember—don't waggle your fingers in the water!

Toothy devil

The name "piranha" comes from native languages in Brazil. It means "tooth fish" or "devil fish."

Large eyes see well over short distances

Sharp teeth for slicing flesh

Powerful jaws for biting

Piranhas grow to about 1 ft (0.3 m) maximum.

Slippery customers: frogs

The creepy-looking African clawed frog is covered in protective slime. It's more slippery than a bar of soap. If it escapes, just try catching it!

Frogs and toads are **amphibians**. They live partly in water and partly on land. A pet African clawed frog needs a tank of clean, fresh water.

The water should be shallow so the frog can stand on the bottom and reach up to breathe air.

Jumpy

Frogs jump. One South African frog did a triple jump of more than 33 ft (10 m)! Make sure the tank has a secure lid so a pet frog can't escape.

amphibian slimy animal with a backbone that lives both in water and on land

Large upward-looking eyes for spotting food

Body covered in mucus (slime) to stop the skin from drying out

Slimy skin puts off predators—it makes the frog hard to grab

Clawed front legs for grabbing food and stuffing it into the mouth

Powerful webbed hind feet for swimming

Quite a mouthful: pythons

Before you buy a pet snake, check how large it will become!

Burmese python catching a rabbit

In Florida, some people buy baby Burmese pythons as pets. Then they discover that the snakes grow to 6.5 feet (2 meters) long in one year. Some owners can't cope, and they release them into the wild. The pythons grow even bigger—up to 23 feet (7 meters) long. They're big enough to swallow alligators!

How dangerous?

Out of about 3,000 kinds of snakes, only around one in ten are venomous (poisonous). Of these, fewer than 100 are dangerous to people.

suffocates   dies from lack of air

The Burmese python coils around its prey, squeezing it tightly. The prey can no longer breathe. It **suffocates** and dies. The python swallows the animal head first. Its jaws and stomach stretch to make room for the enormous meal.

The royal python is a popular pet. For a python, it is small. Like other pythons, it is not venomous.

In the wild, the mottled pattern **breaks up** the python's outline on the forest floor.

When frightened, the snake rolls itself into a tight ball.

This python grows to about 5 ft (1.5 m).

Toothy smiles: crocs

A crocodile has a long snout. You can see the fourth lower tooth when its jaw is shut.

How would you like to find a crocodile in your bathtub? Surprisingly, some people used to keep crocodiles and alligators. Their toothy bite made them dangerous pets.

The Nile crocodile is a feared, meat-eating animal found in many African countries. Crocodiles can float with only their eyes and nostrils showing above the water. This makes them hard to spot.

Going, going ...

Of 23 types of **crocodilians**, four are likely to die out within a few years, unless people take action to save them.

crocodilian   a crocodile, alligator, or caiman

The American alligator lives in Florida's Everglades National Park.

Snout shorter than a crocodile's

Scales protect the skin

When threatened, it opens its mouth **wide** and hisses. This is enough to scare most attackers away!

Webbed feet for swimming

This baby spectacled caiman will grow to about 6.5 ft (2 m). It is sometimes kept as a pet. Watch your fingers!

Not so birdbrained!

Imagine your mom or dad has an important visitor over and suddenly a voice calls out, "Hey, ugly!"—or something much worse! You can blame it on the parrot.

Hey, ugly!

Birdbrained means "stupid," but some birds are far from stupid. A scientist in Arizona taught her grey parrot Alex to recognize and ask for more than 50 different things.

Be careful what you teach your bird! It will copy your voice and your words. Parrots like to mimic sounds—everything from doorbells, to telephone rings, to burps and farts, to barking dogs.

A grey parrot can live for 50 years. Parrots have their own personalities, just like people do.

Deadly dangers

Some common things around the house or garden are deadly to parrots. Avocados and buttercup or rhubarb leaves are poisonous. Tobacco smoke is, too.

The parrot tears off a piece of cooked bone with its bill.

Upper bill used for
hooking
branches or perch when climbing

Point of lower bill used for
cracking
seeds and nuts

Four toes for
grasping
its perch

Rats rule

With its sharp teeth, a rat on the loose can nibble your books, gnaw the TV wires, and ruin your best furniture. This is a pet your parents may truly hate.

Wild rats bite and carry diseases. In Europe in the **Middle Ages**, fleas from black rats passed on a disease called bubonic **plague**. Between 1347 and 1351, the plague killed one third of all European people. Wild rats also carry diseases in their urine and droppings.

Fast breeder!

A female rat can produce 6–12 babies every few weeks. If all her babies survive and breed, she will leave behind 1,000 rats in a year.

For the priests at a temple in Deshnok, India, the rats are holy. The priests care for the rats and even share their feeding bowls. If a visitor accidentally hurts a rat, he or she must pay the priests in gold or silver.

In the Deshnok temple, India, 20,000 rats run free.

Middle Ages the time between the 5th and 15th centuries

People keep pet rats in cages.

Rats can **gnaw** through most things.

Rats need food and water every day.

The cage should be cleaned out once a week.

Eeeek!

Pet rats are tame breeds of the wild brown rat.
They are cleaner and safer than wild rats.

plague a fast-spreading disease that kills people

Ferreting around

Ferrets live life in the fast lane. In the wild, they are a blur of fur. Kept as pets, these sleek bundles of energy demand lots of attention.

Small ears fold back to help the ferret slide easily through burrows.

Ferrets make **dens** in burrows, which they steal from rabbits or dig themselves.

Sharp claws for digging and fast running

Inside the mouth are sharp teeth that can bite through metal.

den shelter

Ferrets need exercise. Some owners race them against other ferrets.

A ferret is a tame European polecat, a type of weasel. In the wild, polecats chase rats, mice, and rabbits. They even attack animals larger than themselves. After catching their prey, they give it a "kill bite" on the neck.

A pet ferret is quite a handful! It can be dangerous if not properly trained and should be kept in a strong cage. If a ferret escapes, it can attack other pets and even babies.

Hide and seek

Ferrets need to explore and play. They should be let out for two to three hours each day. Watch out! Ferrets will hunt down all kinds of things—such as socks and keys—and hide them.

Hogging the limelight

The actor George Clooney used to live with a pot-bellied pig called **Max**. The pig came on film shoots with **George**, and sometimes even slept in his bed!

A pot-bellied pig looks cute when young, but it grows to become heavier than a man.

Thick skin with sparse hairs

enclosure piece of land with a fence or wall around it

There was a craze for pot-bellied pigs in the 1960s and 1970s. Some were bought for thousands of dollars. Many were later given away to pig **sanctuaries** when they grew too big.

Max once went for a ride in actor John Travolta's plane; so pigs do, in fact, fly. Max, weighing in at about 300 pounds (135 kilograms), died in 2006 at the age of 18.

Pooh!

An adult pig produces more than 1 gallon (3–4 liters) of urine and droppings each day.

If overfed, a pot-bellied pig becomes flabby, gets arthritis (the joints become sore), and folds of fat cover the eyes.

A pot-bellied pig has to be kept outdoors. The **enclosure** must have a strong fence—or the pig will bash it down and escape.

sanctuary place where wild animals are protected